WRITE THE DAMN BOOK!

Steps For Overcoming Your Fear of Writing

Stefanie Newell

Write One Publications, LLC

Copyright © 2022 by Stefanie Newell

Write One Publications, LLC
www.howtowriteabookthatsells.com

Write The Damn Book! / Stefanie Newell – 1st ed.

ISBN: 978-0-9821484-9-5

This book is meant to be interactive. Please be ready to jot down answers to the questions.

http://howtowriteabookthatsells.com

—STEFANIE NEWELL

CONTENTS

CHAPTER ONE

Introduction

So let me guess... you have an idea for a book, and even though it's incessantly nagging at you, you just can't begin writing your manuscript. Perhaps you doubt your writing ability and think, "What if I'm not good enough?"

Or maybe you're stuck in an endless loop of questions like: Who am I to write a book? Will I be able to come up with enough content? What if my outline isn't good or my research isn't sufficient? What if people judge me? Or worse yet, tell me my writing sucks?

And then, finally, after a mental tug-of-war, you resign yourself to the fact that writing a book isn't for you.

You tell yourself, "I'm no Stephen King," and then decide that writing is one less goal to concern yourself with.

I've just described what I like to refer to as the literary equivalent of stage fright. A fear so crippling that you either never start your manuscript, or you do start your manuscript but never actually publish it.

Can I let you in on a little secret? You're not alone. The fear of writing is common. So common, that it's the first obstacle aspiring writers usually have to conquer. Fear has an uncanny way of rearing its ugly head as soon as you make the declaration, "I want to write a book!"

You might have had a desire to write since an early age. Or maybe there was a life event that compelled you to want to share your story. Perhaps you're an expert and your knowledge of a particular subject has your audience practically begging you to write a book. Whatever the reason, once you've been called to write, that nagging feeling will never go away.

And that's why I want to help you to fulfill your dream of becoming a published author! I've encountered so many people who've expressed their desire to write but don't know the steps to take to move past their fear and begin writing.

In this book, I'll be sharing my publishing journey - which I must tell you - fear was front and center for. I will also help you to identify exactly what your fears are, as well as provide you with actionable steps that you can take right now to begin writing.

I can't assure you that you won't experience the fear of writing ever again. But what I can tell you is this: if you make a sincere effort to conquer your writing fears through the exercises I provide in this book, in the next 12 months, you'll finally be able to call yourself a published author.

So, if you're ready to look fear in the face and be transparent, let's begin to get real so that you can accomplish your dream of becoming a published author!

CHAPTER TWO

Life Opens Up When You Do

> *"The master has failed more times than the beginner has even tried." – Stephen McCranie*

Fourteen years ago, while sitting in a cubicle, I decided that my 9 to 5 was no longer serving me. So I began visualizing what I wanted my career to look like and expressed my desire to become a published author to my closest confidants. I could no longer ignore the strong urge to follow my passion for becoming a published author.

I'll be the first to admit; initially, I only saw a writing career in my future. I had no idea that starting my manuscript would turn into me becoming a writing coach.

I've been writing since I was a little girl, so writing a book was just a natural progression in a long line of other creative writing experiences I'd had. In my twenties, I'd written numerous poems and short stories, penned a song that was sung by an independent artist, and another that was featured in an independent film. I'd even begun an entertainment blog and gotten my dream job moonlighting as a freelance writer for an entertainment magazine.

So, the writing itself never really scared me, but sharing that writing was a different story.

For over two years, I worked on penning my debut novel, *The Buzz: When Celebrity Gossip Goes Wrong*, while I still worked in corporate America. In 2008 in the middle of the economic downturn, I was laid off. It was then that I had to decide. Was I going to continue the corporate career path I'd been on? Or would I step out on faith and pursue a full-time writing career?

Ultimately, I decided to find a new corporate position. I did, however, continue with my literary pursuits.

After finishing my manuscript, one of the first steps in the publishing process was sending the manuscript to an editor. This was quite possibly the scariest thing I'd ever encountered. What if she didn't get my writing? What if she didn't think it was good enough?

So, I waited the three longest weeks of my life for her to return my edited manuscript back to me. Days felt like years. And after three long weeks, do you know what she said? She said she loved it!

It felt like I hadn't breathed in those three weeks, but the day I received my manuscript back, I could finally exhale. Someone had read every page of my writing and loved it.

After that boost of confidence, the self-publishing process was finally underway. Having secured a new position in corporate America, I was ready to take on the publishing world.

A few weeks into my new role, I figured maybe I wasn't so tired of corporate after all. Pursuing my goal of becoming a published writer had even improved my days at work. The job change had also invigorated me, and I was starting to think I might have just needed a new environment.

Unfortunately, that feeling was short-lived. The company was in financial trouble. Some months later, I was laid off again. It was almost as if the universe was saying, "No, it's really time for you to move on."

I'd always wanted to write full-time, but I wasn't sure I wanted to leave my corporate job to pursue it. But when the second layoff happened, I didn't need any more urging. I knew what I had to do. I decided that I wasn't going to play it safe anymore. I was going to go after my dream of becoming a full-time writer.

I didn't know exactly how that would happen or what that would even mean regarding salary, but I knew that I needed to take the first step and publish my book.

I was scared. I'm talking, teeth chattering, knees knocking, scared. I had a car payment, mortgage, a child in private school, and every other expense that adults incur. And, of course, the inner critic in me started again. What if my book doesn't sell? Am I really that good of a writer?

These were all thoughts I had before sending my book off to reviewers, book clubs, and the media in preparation for the launch date of my book.

Have you ever been waiting for something really important to come in the mail? Day after day, you anxiously check the mailbox, and on the day when it finally shows up, you don't want to open it?

Well, that's how I felt when the reviews started to roll in for my book. I was so afraid to click on the emails that I wouldn't have opened any of them if I could. But I did…

One by one, I read each and every review. All of the reviewers said they loved my book. In the following months, my book was featured in magazines, including Rolling Out and J'adore Magazine. I was featured in a newspaper, recognized by my alma mater, asked to be a part of online radio shows and the morning news in Chicago, and visited multiple cities for book signings.

Because of my very first book, I was eventually able to share my self-publishing journey with other aspiring writers. I can't even articulate how this made me feel. I couldn't believe that little ole me - the person who stepped out on faith and went after her dream - was inspiring others to do the same thing.

As a result, I started speaking at writing conferences, including the Bronzeville Film Festival, National Black Book Conference, and the Los Angeles Book Expo. And this eventually led to me starting my coaching business. The rest is, as they say, history.

Had I allowed fear to stop me from going after my dream, I wouldn't have had the joy of saying that I was a published author or a writing coach.

I share my publishing experience with you because I think it's vital for aspiring writers to understand that fear crosses practically everyone's mind when they embark upon something great.

What significant accomplishments have you had in your life where fear wasn't attached? You probably can't think of one. With your past accomplishments, how did you handle your fears? Did you move past them? If you did move past them, did everything end up okay? And do you regret not going after your goals if you didn't?

Everything I've encountered in my personal and professional life has scared me and caused me to grow.

If I told you that it's been fourteen years since I published my first book, and I still get fearful, would you believe me? Well, I do. Even while writing this book, the self-deprecating chatter started.

Why do you think YOU have the experience to write on fear? You're a writing coach! Who's going to want to hear this coming from you? Do you even have a solution?

And to shut fear up, I told it: "I can write on fear because I deal with it often."

The only thing that separates me from others is that I don't allow fear to consume me to the point of being paralyzed. I don't focus on fear. I focus on my goals. And I think it's important that you do the same.

Now let's be clear… The fact that I continue to move past my fear doesn't mean that I haven't made a ton of mistakes, experienced pitfalls, had disappointments, or had nights where I thought, "Why the hell did you leave all that stability?"

What has kept me going is that I don't want to live my life with regrets. I also know that every other successful person who's had a goal or a dream has experienced the same fears I'm encountering.

If they could accomplish their goals despite the fear, why not me? I'm worthy of achieving my goals, right?

Imagine all the things you wouldn't have accomplished in your life if you'd let fear stop you. Would you have gone to college? Gotten married? Had kids? Gotten on a plane to travel the world? So why is writing different? Why does writing bring about this type of fear?

I believe that writing is different because it's something that's creative and requires you to be completely transparent with the world. No matter what genre you write, the sharing of your personal thoughts is scary.

While we've been taught how to write generally, we've not all been taught the nuances of literature. Or how to develop characters and plots. Or about the publishing industry, book marketing, and sales…

But everything in life is an education, right? Don't let fear stop you because you have little to no knowledge of writing or publishing.

The truth is, my degree is in finance. All of my work experience is in finance. But my time in corporate America was valuable and needed for my publishing journey to happen and, ironically, for it to succeed.

Everything I know about writing has been self-taught. I had a general idea of what I needed to do before writing my book, but I can't tell you the number of tireless nights I spent researching everything. I researched writing, marketing, and publishing. And to this day, I still invest that same amount of time and energy into learning my craft.

If you're reading this book, you likely have some fear. However, I think it's important that you're also honest about what exactly is making you fearful.

Is it fear of not being good enough, fear of failure, fear of success, or fear of judgment? In the next chapter, I challenge you to figure out what's at the root of your fear so that you can conquer it. Are you ready? Well, let's begin.

The Truth Is… You're Good Enough!

> *"If you want to be a writer, you must do two things above all others: read a lot and write a lot. There's no way around these two things that I'm aware of, no shortcut." – Stephen King*

Fear is prevalent in just about every writer, singer, actor, and performer of the arts. Despite being in a profession that requires them to be in front of large groups of people, singer Brandy, actress Megan Fox, and the legendary Barbara Streisand all struggle with fear. So consider yourself in good company.

There are many different reasons why aspiring writers struggle with fear. Hopefully, you'll figure out which of these fears resonates with you the most. I believe that understanding where your fear is rooted will help you to move past it.

The most common reason I hear aspiring writers profess a fear of writing is that they don't believe their writing is good enough. And believe me, I understand where this fear comes from. But the truth is, your writing will not improve until you begin to write more.

Yes, it's true. Some aspiring writers are naturally inclined to write, while others must invest a little more time to hone their craft.

However, it's through continual writing and reading, as well as allowing others to critique your writing, that you discover your strengths and weaknesses. So how do you become a better writer?

Well, there are two ways to become a better writer. One of the most important investments you can make in your writing career is making time to read the genre you aspire to write in. This act alone will help you to improve your writing.

Good writers are avid readers! Exposure to other authors, especially literary greats, will help you discover aspects of your writing that you need to develop.

Identifying what you like in others' writing will significantly benefit you when you begin to write your own manuscript. This will give you a clearer vision of what appeals to you so you can develop those strengths in your writing. If your concern is whether your writing is good enough, let me be the first to tell you that this will always be a concern, no matter how many books you publish.

Don't allow the fear of your writing not being good enough to stop you from writing!

Ironically, in my experience as a writing coach, every person I've ever encountered who felt like they weren't good enough were all fantastic writers. Let that soak in for a minute...

Some of the best writers I've encountered didn't think they were good enough! Even to this day, I experience writing sessions where I sit down and begin reading my own manuscript, and I think, "Whoa, this is amazing!" And then, two hours later, I come back and read the same passage and think to myself, "Wow, this sucks!"

My point is: there will always be a concern about whether your writing is good enough or not. Depending on the day and your mood, you might think your writing is Pulitzer Prize-winning. On another day, you may feel like you should be ashamed for even wasting time writing. And to be clear, I'm speaking about reading the same passage of writing!

Again, push yourself to continue to write! It's the only way your writing will ever improve.

The second way to become a better writer is by learning to accept constructive criticism and implement the suggestions provided.

Sharing your writing with others leaves you extremely vulnerable, which might be where some of your fear stems from. I expressed in the last chapter how sending my manuscript to my editor was one of the hardest things I subjected myself to while publishing my first book. However, my editor's feedback helped my manuscript get to the point where readers could say that my book was good.

Every part of the writing process will require you to be vulnerable. From writing to editing to publishing, you will consistently expose yourself and be pushed well outside your comfort zone. If you're sensitive about your writing to the point of nobody being able to critique you in any way, then you're doing yourself a great disservice.

Singer Erykah Badu said it best when she said, "I'm an artist, and I'm sensitive about my shit."

I believe it's perfectly okay to be sensitive about your writing. In fact, I think it's normal.

However, it's important that you learn how to accept critiques. It's also vital to understand that everyone won't like your writing. And they're within reason to feel that way. Understanding this will help you to not take it so personally when someone critiques your book. Depending on exactly whom that critique is coming from, it will be your responsibility to separate what actually needs to be improved and what is simply just an opinion.

As a writing coach, I can tell you that I always have my client's best interest at heart. When I provide developmental editing, my intent is to always help the writer to get to the best possible version of their final draft.

If you've elected someone to act as your beta reader, editor, or writing coach and they don't make you feel safe sharing your writing with them, delegate a new person! If they don't get your writing, delegate a new person! Having a sense of security that this person understands your writing and is only making suggestions to ensure you become the best writer will be essential to your success and growth.

Lastly, when reviewing critiques or suggestions, don't become overwhelmed! I've seen this repeatedly happen when a writer becomes so overwhelmed with the comments that they either don't implement any of the suggestions and publish anyway or stop writing altogether. Both of these actions can be costly mistakes.

The easiest way to handle feedback is to break the suggestions down into easily digestible sections so that you can work on improving your manuscript one step at a time. In fact, the entire art of writing a manuscript can be overcome one small step at a time.

In conclusion, if the writing makes you fearful, you need to read and write more. If the sharing of your writing is something that makes you nervous, know that it is a necessary part of the process.

Every step in the publishing process, from beta readers, to editors, to writing coaches, to book reviewers to your readers themselves, requires you to share your writing.

I want to help you to move past the fear of someone reading and critiquing your writing. But for now, I want you to start identifying your writing strengths and weaknesses on the following workbook page.

What do you consider your strengths and weaknesses as far as writing is concerned?

____

____

____

____

____

____

____

____

What aspects of your favorite writer's books do you enjoy?

Fiction writers, ask yourself this of your favorite writers:

- ➢ How do they introduce characters?
- ➢ Do they write in first person or third?
- ➢ How do they pace their book?
- ➢ How do they create internal and external conflict?
- ➢ How do they develop their plots and sub-plots?
- ➢ What do you enjoy about their writing style?

____

____

____

____

____

____

And for non-fiction writers, ask this of your favorite writer:

> ➤ How does your favorite writer introduce their subject matter?
> ➤ Do you enjoy books that motivate, provide history, or books that are inspirational?
> ➤ What is the pacing of their book?

____

____

____

____

____

____

What do you enjoy about their writing voice?

CHAPTER FOUR

You Too Can Write A Book!

> *"Man is not worried by real problems, so much as by his imagined anxieties about real problems."* - Epictetus

Some aspiring writers question their ability to pen a book because they aren't college-educated, are too old, too young, a blogger, scared they'll be exposed as a fraud, only have one book in them, or English isn't their first language.

While these may seem logical reasons for not writing a book, these are just detractors that have no relevance as to whether you can write a book or not.

The truth is, these may very well have been great excuses 10 or 15 years ago. However, how we consume information now, as well as who we consume information from, has changed. Even children are writing books now!

Think about the spiritual gurus, relationship, fitness, and health experts that have cropped up. What about platforms like blogs or YouTube, where people garner millions of views on subjects ranging from makeup to gaming?

The time is now to share what you know. It doesn't matter what your age is, how you made the transition to writing, or whether you're educated traditionally - write a book if you have something of value to say!

Now with that being said, I think it's also important to note that while anyone is capable of writing a book, there are still expectations from the readers.

With non-fiction writers, there is an expectation that you be an expert or have extensive knowledge of the subject matter you're writing on.

Am I saying that because you don't have a college degree or some type of certification that this genre is closed off to you? No, not at all. I'm saying that you need to know what you're talking about – period.

Are you an expert? If so, what makes you one? Do you have extensive knowledge of the genre you write? If so, where did you garner that knowledge?

Answering this will not only help you to write without having to silence your inner critic, but it will also help you to present your book to your audience in a way that allows them to trust and relate to you.

An example that I often like to use is Steve Harvey's *Act Like A Lady, Think Like A Man.*

Is Steve Harvey a relationship expert? His area of expertise, in my opinion, would be comedy. So how has a relationship book penned by a comedian sold over two million copies worldwide?

Steve Harvey became a bestseller because he never presented himself as an expert. Instead, he presented his ideas as a man who has had two failed marriages and been in several relationships, and based on his experiences, he feels this is what it takes to snag a man.

Love him or hate him, his Uncle Steve approach worked. And because of this, he's been able to follow his first book up with *Straight Talk, No Chaser: How to Find and Keep a Man.*

So how do you use this same strategy when crafting your book? If you don't have the "expert" moniker to back you up, make your audience aware of who you are and why you're qualified to write on the subject matter in the introduction of your book.

For example, suppose you have a health condition and want to write a book on how you were able to holistically heal that condition. In that case, you may not have the education or expertise to back you up; instead, you have the experience.

So in the introduction of your book, you should explain to your target audience exactly who you are and why you decided to write a book. You can also include this in your book description when you publish it.

By way of experience, you have extensive knowledge of the subject and are, therefore, qualified to share information. By not angling yourself as an expert and presenting yourself to your reader as someone who has "been there and done that," don't you think in some ways that would make you more relatable?

Depending on where the reader is in their journey, they may be completely over the idea of traditional medicine and its methods for healing the condition. You may be the breath of fresh air this person is looking for.

The fact that you aren't a doctor may be more appealing because now the reader knows that you're relatable and have actually experienced what they're going through, not just spewing statistics and data.

Now I must strongly caution you to stay in your lane. If you're not an expert, then be mindful of giving medical, legal, or financial advice. You can speak on your own experiences, but you won't be in a position to advise someone else as to what they should do.

Dr. Phil, for example, can provide advice to his readers in a way that Steve Harvey cannot. Understanding your lane is very important as it relates to credibility among your audience.

For bloggers looking to transition into becoming an author, don't let yourself or the naysayers stop you from your goal.

Some of the scrutiny bloggers experience is related to journalists and professional writers being upset that their territories are being encroached upon. While others are upset because some bloggers are not respecting the writing craft and share information that is not based on facts, is not well written or is just flat-out libelous.

We've all seen the occasional article pop up that gets steam and goes viral, and then you find out that the news article is completely unfounded.

The best way to combat someone being able to say, "Oh, you're only a blogger," or, "Stick to blogging," is to know your shit! I really don't know any other way to say it.

By researching and testing your ideas, give your readers confidence that you know what you're talking about!

You should also present your topic in a format appropriate for your publishing platform.

For example, there are some bloggers who are copying their blog posts and then turning them into a book without making the book consistent with publishing standards. Is there anything wrong with this? Not necessarily, but you must know and understand the platform you're selling on.

I've seen this work very well for bloggers who are selling PDF eBooks from their own blogging platform. Their audience in general will be more accepting of this format because of the platform that they're selling it from.

However, as a writing coach, I would still encourage you to present those types of eBooks consistent with publishing standards even if you're selling them from your own platform. I would also suggest you provide additional information that isn't readily available on your blog. This way your reader, whether they are familiar with your platform or not, will see you as an author and not only as a blogger. By presenting your content professionally, you're also setting yourself up to be offered opportunities like speaking engagements, media opportunities, or the ability to coach.

As a blogger, you must understand that Amazon is a whole other beast. Their audience has a completely different set of expectations for the authors who publish on their platform. The readers expect the book to be laid out in a book format and be written in a certain style. You should absolutely cater to their expectations, if not exceed them.

This will require you to create your book in the format they're accustomed to. So, for example, instead of simply copying and pasting, you'll need to create an introduction and rework blog posts so that they are presented more like chapters and less like a blog post. You'll also need to write a conclusion and be mindful of pacing and writing style.

These, of course, are just the basics. Your goal as a writer should always be to provide value. You may find that simply cutting and pasting popular blog posts may not be valuable to the reader at all. Especially when you are selling content and not giving it away for free.

If you determine that your non-fiction book does not provide value, you'll need to consider how you can meet the expectation of your target reader.

For some bloggers, your writing voice itself may concern you. I would encourage you to look at your blog as what has allowed you to hone your distinctive writing voice. This is essentially your personality coming through the page, and you need this in writing to not write one monotone chapter after another.

Blogging has an uncanny way of making you present your ideas authentically. As such, it allows each of us to have a unique writing voice that's all our own.

My writing voice has always been very conversational, much like if you were talking to me in person. I've tried other writing voices, and none of them ever felt comfortable. Through consistent blogging, I was finally able to develop my voice.

Now, of course, my writing voice changes a bit when I'm writing fiction. However, blogging has allowed me to determine the style of writing that I enjoy when delivering information to my non-fiction readers.

And remember - your writing voice should be consistent across all platforms. It should carry from your blog to your book to your social media. No matter what piece of writing of yours I read, I should know that it came from you.

The best example of writing voice I like to use is Tyler Perry. If you're familiar with his plays, movies, and TV shows, you probably don't need an explanation as to what I'm talking about. He has a very distinct writing voice. Not only is it present in his film endeavors but also in his emails and social media posts. So much so when I open an email from him, all I can hear is his voice (or even Madea's). That's how consistent your writing voice should be too.

If your blogging voice has hindered your transition into becoming a published author, know that your audience has come to love and appreciate your unique voice. Give your readers what they've grown to love about your writing, including your voice.

If age is your concern, consider your audience. If you're a younger writer, be mindful of your target audience and present your information accordingly. For example, I recently read a blog post from a 16-year-old that's making $5,000 a month running successful Internet businesses. As far as I can tell, his target audience is adults. Yet, for the most part, no one seemed turned off by the fact that the information was coming from a teenager.

Why? Because he knows his subject matter inside and out, and he shares exactly who he is and why he's qualified to write on the subject in the introduction of his blog. And lastly, he stays in his lane and writes what he knows. He's not presenting information that requires him to have life experience. Instead, he's presenting information on businesses he's been successful in. Who can deny that?

When presenting your subject matter, keep your audience's age in mind.

I don't want relationship advice from a teenager. But perhaps I'd be more open to a teenager teaching me how to set up my WordPress blog or how to grow a social media following. Again, be mindful of your audience.

If you are older, just know there's no expiration date for writing and publishing a book. As a matter of fact, for certain genres, I would much prefer the author to be older because there is value in hearing the wisdom of the older generation. In fact, a small percentage of my clients are 70 years old or older.

If you feel that your lack of education is a problem, there are many resources on Amazon and the Internet that will get you up to speed on what you need to learn. Don't discount being self-taught! In some instances, being self-taught will allow you to learn even more intensely about the subject you're passionate about. If your concern is not knowing where to start, I can assure you that I have many resources to get you on the right track. Remember, your first step is to start writing.

Some aspiring writers experience what is called imposter syndrome. Imposter syndrome was coined in 1978 by clinical psychologists Dr. Pauline R. Clance and Suzanne A. Imes. Imposter syndrome refers to high-achieving individuals marked by an inability to internalize their accomplishments and a persistent fear of being exposed as a "fraud."

One of my clients experienced imposter syndrome soon after publishing her first book. She began to feel as though she couldn't accept the credit for the success her book received. She felt like people would discover that she was a fraud and had no idea what she was talking about.

Now, of course, all of this was unfounded because not only did she have the education, but she also had the life and work experience to back her up.

My point is, don't let self-deprecation rile you up. The human mind often creates problems that don't even exist. Not only has no one ever "found" her out, but she's been publicly lauded for her book.

Another prevalent concern I hear from aspiring writers is that they feel they only have one book in them. To that, I say, so what if you do?

Is that so bad? Maybe one book is all that's needed to take your business or your blog to the next level, to begin getting speaking engagements or to begin coaching, or to just say you did it!

Everyone is not meant to be a full-time writer. Some will publish a book because they feel inspired, while others will make a career out of writing.

The truth is there's no right or wrong way to be an author. Do what works best for you! Above all else, if you desire to write, whether it's one book or hundreds, you have to start by writing the first book.

You won't know whether a career is an option until you dip your toe in the water. I knew I wanted to write, but I didn't fully understand how much I wanted and needed to write until I published my first book. And I had the same concern.

What if I only have one book in me?

And here I am fourteen books later… The truth is you won't run out of ideas. There probably isn't a professional writer alive that has run out of ideas. Fear may inhibit you, but running out of ideas should never be a concern.

If you're concerned about a language barrier, you must write consistently to build your confidence. Once your final draft is completed, you'll need to hire an editor. With your editor's help, you'll learn the nuances of the language and, over time, become better at writing.

No matter what your fear is, the number one thing you need to do is silence your inner critic. There isn't an obstacle you can come up with that doesn't have a solution. Now that I've knocked down all your barriers, can we agree to just write the damn book already?

CHAPTER FIVE

What Is The Purpose Of Fear?

> *"It is impossible to live without failing at something, unless you live so cautiously that you might as well have not lived at all, in which case you have failed by default." – J.K. Rowling*

What if fear wasn't a part of your life? Is it possible that fear is one of the things that defines our character? What if fear was the reality check we needed to determine if we really wanted the goal we've professed to be so passionate about?

Of course, it's really easy to look at fear as a negative. However, I would argue there's a reason why we have been equipped with this mechanism to begin with.

When I think back on my own life, I have always been a bit of a risk-taker. Even as a teenage girl, I would go after my dreams in a way that I noticed others my age weren't. That didn't mean I wasn't scared. It just meant that I didn't care what the risks were. If I failed, so what? Failure wouldn't kill me; it would only make me stronger.

As an adult, the fear went from a whisper to being louder in the recesses of my mind. Perhaps this may be your experience too.

As children, we're usually told that we can do and become anything we want, so we're usually less fearful at this stage. As adults, we have more responsibilities (financial and otherwise). We've begun experiencing failures, had people tell us no, and in some cases, had people outright try and talk us out of our dreams.

As a result, we tend to give more thought to our fears than we did when we were younger. I know I do, but I am still very much the person who, despite fear, takes risks and just goes for it.

After leaving my corporate position and starting my writing career, I moved from Chicago to Georgia. I did this not knowing a lot of people in the city I was moving to and fresh in the throes of becoming a full-time writer. I decided to move because it was something I'd wanted to do for a while. I needed to experience something new and different, and I wasn't going to allow fear to stop me.

And guess what? Everything worked out. Did everything work out perfectly? Not exactly. But had I not taken that plunge, much of what has become available to me - the opportunities, the growth in my business, and the life experiences I've gained - wouldn't have happened.

With that being said, you know yourself better than I do, and by now, you should be more aware of your fears. I encourage you to always be authentic when acknowledging those fears and hold true to what feels right. To be clear, I'm not suggesting you quit your job and write full-time without a plan. I'm suggesting that you have confidence that you can become a published author.

Everyone is not meant to throw caution to the wind as I have, but what's stopping you from writing your manuscript when you get home from your full-time job, while your kids are down for a nap, or when you have spare time? If not now, when? If not you, who?

Perhaps you haven't given much thought to your fears in the past, but I encourage you to think about what's truly at the core of your fear.

While in the context of this book, we're talking about your fear of writing, I think there's value in questioning where all of your other fears stem from too. Is it a fear of failure?

Fear of failure is very common, and I've had several clients express that they are scared to publish because they don't know if their book will do well. Let's ease your fears some.

Within publishing, the best way to set yourself up against failure is through education. This means understanding the needs of your target audience, understanding the components of a successful book, having a well-thought-out marketing plan, and having realistic expectations of what will come from publishing a book.

It's important to note that true writing success comes with proper planning and having a good understanding of all of the areas of the publishing industry for you to succeed. While the publishing industry is about writing, it's also about business. So it's just as important that you understand publishing, marketing, and branding, as much as you do the writing.

For aspiring writers who don't properly plan they wait until their manuscript is complete or their book is published before they start giving thoughts to these business areas. This is when you are at a greater risk of failure. The time to be concerned with these areas is when you are still writing your manuscript. The idea is that you learn your strengths and weaknesses before publishing and exposing yourself to your readers. Consider the questions on the following workbook page to put this into perspective.

What are your goals as a writer?

I want to increase my social media following on the following platform:

____

What do you need to know about sales, branding, and social media in order to accomplish your goal?

____

____

____

____

____

Do you plan to self-publish or traditionally publish?

____

What do you need to know about this publishing method in order to publish?

____

____

____

____

____

____

Do you write fiction or non-fiction?

____

What genre do you write?

____

What do you need to know about your genre in order to publish?

____

____

____

What are the challenges you are currently facing (if any)?

Do you have a social media presence? Yes or no.

What is your level of expertise on social media? Novice? Intermediate? Experienced?

What do you need to learn to get from where you are to where you need to be on social media?

By answering the questions on the previous pages, you will begin to understand the areas to which you need to start giving more attention.

For example, if you chose traditional publishing as your publishing method, how much do you understand about this process? Do you know how long it takes to publish your book when you go this route? Have you begun thinking about a possible agent for your book? A possible publishing house for your book?

You decrease your chances of failure by considering the areas in which you need to increase your education. Now let's also talk about what is considered a failure concerning publishing your first book.

Let me start by saying that some aspiring writers have unrealistic expectations of what constitutes success for their first book. Some feel as though writers don't make any money. Then others are on the opposite side of the spectrum and believe they'll be able to quit their jobs after publishing one book. And while that may be true for a tiny percentage of writers, that's simply not the case for most of us.

There's a saying in the publishing industry that goes, "Nothing sells book one like book two. Nothing sells book two, like book three." This is true for several reasons:

> - You gain more experience with each book and begin to write better.
> - You begin to understand the formula for successful books.
> - You begin to grow a readership for your books.
> - You have a greater sense of your target audience's expectations.

So, in general, what is considered to be a publishing success? Well, I can't answer this definitively because many different tangible and non-tangible factors determine whether a book is successful.

Again, the first question would be: What are your personal goals? The answer will be different for each person. And keep in mind there's no right or wrong answer where this is concerned. However, as a word of caution for new writers, don't let the number of books you sell be your only determining factor for success.

For example, suppose your goal is to advance your career to get speaking engagements. In that case, the number of books you sell may not be as significant as the opportunities that are afforded to you as a result of becoming a published author.

When thinking about non-tangible factors, consider the following:

> How have you grown your social media following as a result of writing your book? How has writing a book affected how your audience sees your brand?

> What opportunities have been awarded to you as a result of your book? (i.e., interviews, speaking engagements, media and consulting opportunities, etc.)

> If your book is sold on your own platform, how has your book increased your website traffic? Has it increased exposure to resources like your blog, courses, and other products?

> ➤ For non-fiction writers, how has your book helped you establish yourself as an expert on the subject matter you write?

As far as tangible factors, consider the following:

> ➤ How much money have you spent on publishing your book? Consider all of your publishing costs.
> ➤ How many books will you need to sell, and what will they be priced at to recoup your initial investment?

When considering the tangible factors, you must also be mindful of the platform you sell your book on. As I said, there are two different expectations depending on the platform your book is published on.

For example, here are some things to note if you sell your book on Amazon:

> ➤ They are the most extensive book retailer on the Internet; thus, they provide you with exposure to their audience.
> ➤ Certain genres can be very competitive and require consistent sales to rank and do well.
> ➤ You can use Amazon SEO to garner even more traffic and sales for your book.
> ➤ Some readers prefer Amazon over making purchases on other book retail sites or personal blogs and websites.
> ➤ Amazon handles all the shipping of your print book or the transmission of your eBook.

- ➤ You are required to price your book competitively on Amazon. eBooks are usually priced at $2.99 and up, while print books typically start at $9.99, depending on the page count.
- ➤ Depending on whether your book is an eBook or print book, you will have a royalty split anywhere from 35% to 70%.
- ➤ You will be paid approximately sixty (60) days following the end of the calendar month in which your royalties meet the payment threshold.

If you sell from your platform:

- ➤ You will draw from your already existing audience. These people are familiar with your brand and are more likely to purchase.
- ➤ You can use SEO to attract search engine traffic to your book.
- ➤ You can price your book based on value and garner a bigger profit.
- ➤ You may find that it may be more challenging to sell fiction.
- ➤ You can work with affiliates and allow them to also sell your book.
- ➤ You can collect the names and email addresses of the people who purchase your book and continue to provide value and sell to them.
- ➤ If you sell a print book, you are responsible for shipping.
- ➤ You will be required to have a shopping cart on your site.

> ➢ You get paid instantly.

As you can see from this exercise, there are many things you need to consider before publishing your book. That's why you should think about this now so as not to put yourself in a position of failure by waiting until after you publish to consider how you will publish.

A well-thought-out plan will help you strategize the best course of action for your book project. Depending on the genre you write, your goals, and your initial investment, this could differ for each person.

If fear of failure is a concern of yours, remember the only way to fail is to not try. Do you want to go through life not having tried something you feel inspired to do? And even with all the planning in the world, if it doesn't go well, it still won't be a failure.

Now some people have the exact opposite fear – a fear of success. And this may be something you're dealing with and not even aware of. The fear of success can halt you in your tracks like the fear of failure.

It's not that the fear of success means the person doesn't want to be successful because they do. However, if success doesn't come easily, subconsciously, the person may begin doing things that could sabotage their success. Those things could include what I like to call the three p's: perfectionism, procrastination, and pitfalls.

Perfectionism is something I struggled with a lot at the beginning of my writing career. Perfectionism rears its ugly head in many ways and can hinder you from completing every step in the publishing process, from writing to publishing and marketing.

I happen to be one of those who believes if I'm going to do something, I'm going to do it to the best of my ability or not do it all. So when I published my first book, it took me a very long time to write "The End" because I needed it to be perfect.

What that meant was writing sessions where I would read and re-read my book over and over again. It was like I was stuck in this loop where I was looking to make sure the flow was perfect, that I was using the right words, that I had provided enough detail and description, that the dialogue was perfect, and on and on it went.

Now that I've been writing for much longer, I know there is no such thing as perfection. Of course, you want to ensure that your book is well-written. However, you will always find something that can be improved upon. So for that reason, you must reach a point where you accept your book as complete.

Since I know this can be an issue, I have a completely different process to prevent myself from going down this road.

When I write, I give myself a completion date and stick to it as closely as possible. I also write until I get my thoughts out and then leave the editing until the end. It's something about self-editing that can send me down the perfectionism rabbit hole. Knowing what can either trigger your perfectionism or hinder you from writing "The End" will help you immensely.

Procrastination is the second "p" and is exactly what it sounds like. Some aspiring writers completely drag their feet and keep putting off until tomorrow what can be done today. These are the people who think, "I'm going to write my book when my kids graduate high school. I'll have more time then."

Or, "I'm going to get around to writing. It's just that I'm so busy at work I can barely find any free time."

Or the dreaded, "I'm going to write the book next year! I'm for real this time."

If this is you, my question is, how bad do you want it? Do you want to be a writer? Do you want to have a published book? Because if you did, you'd realize that if you make temporary sacrifices today, achieving your goal is within reach!

The last and final "p" is pitfalls. This is probably the most common "p" I witness among my clients.

Once they decide that they are going to write their book and begin getting a little momentum, out of nowhere, a pitfall hinders them. Now this in and of itself is not the writer's fault. However, how you choose to handle the pitfall can make or break your writing momentum and is what separates aspiring writers from published ones.

My personal experience is that pitfalls happen when I'm working towards expanding my business. Everything will be going great, and then bam - brick wall!

I'll be doing well and then the algorithm will tank my engagement with my audience. Something will happen in my personal life which may cause me to lose focus. My website might crash, or I delete my entire business folder, and the backup is from three months ago. This week, my Instagram stopped working, and I couldn't figure out why despite much research. I could keep going on and on, but these things have happened to me this year alone.

Now, I can just give up and throw in the towel, or I can keep pressing forward and realize that there will always be something that will require me to revamp my strategy and maybe even backtrack my steps.

When each of these things happened, I kept pressing forward.

Don't be the writer that just gives up and leaves a half-written manuscript on their computer that could very well be a bestseller. Don't be the aspiring writer who never gives themselves a chance at holding their completed book in their hand. And certainly don't sabotage yourself.

There's a viral meme that's been floating around for quite some time, and I believe it sums up what success looks like:

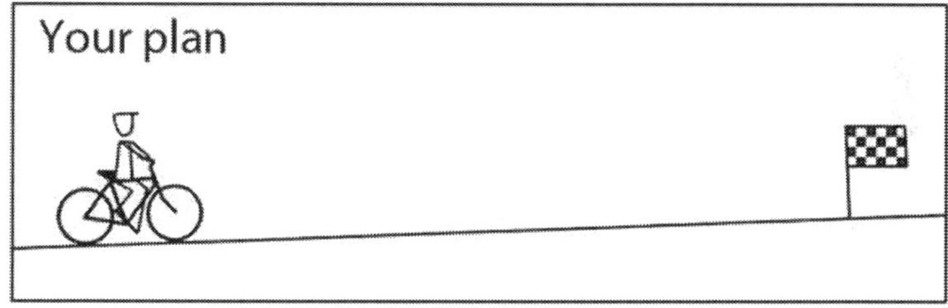

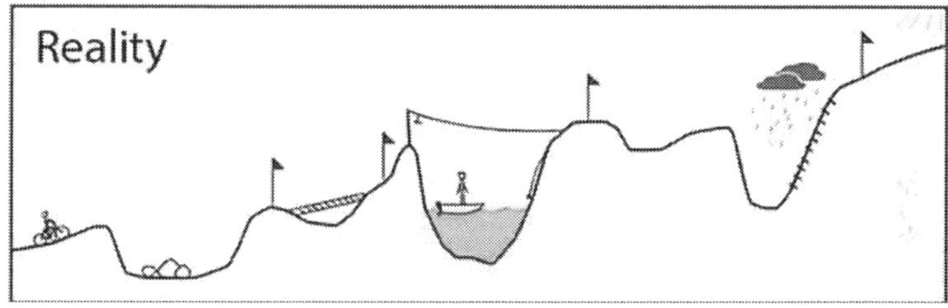

As you can see from the above image, success is not a straight line. You have no idea the opportunities on the other side of your fear. Instead of being fearful of going after success, focus on what success can mean for you.

What will success mean for your life, your career, your self-esteem, and even for your finances?

We've spent a few chapters reviewing the different fears that could hinder you from writing your book. I believe acknowledging your fears puts you in a better position to conquer them. So give it a little thought, and on the next page, I want you to be transparent and identify exactly what your fears are.

Once you've done that, I want to provide you with some actionable steps to help you move past your fears, begin writing your book, and accomplish any goals that make you fearful.

What are your fears?

How do you plan to move past those fears?

What will motivate you to move past your fears?

____

____

____

____

____

____

____

____

Moving Past The Fear

"If you break it down into small steps, you can do any-thing." – Dave Ramsey

Before writing this book, I asked numerous aspiring writers exactly what they needed to overcome their fear of writing. While everyone knew that fear was present, none could articulate exactly what they needed to overcome their fear and begin writing.

So when figuring out what to include in this book, I had to draw from my personal experiences and what motivated me to overcome my fears. Some of those things include a desire to fulfill my goals, and, if I was being honest, simply acknowledging that I enjoy a challenge.

What I will be providing in the coming pages will be what I do to move past fear. It doesn't stop fear from creeping in from time to time.

Instead, it allows you to take small actionable steps toward your goal. While this book was written specifically for writing, you may find that what I'll be sharing will be helpful in any area of your life where fear is present. On the following pages, I will share things not necessarily related to writing but things that have helped me achieve my goals.

Have A Positive Mindset

"Whatever the mind can conceive and believe, it can achieve." - Napoleon Hill

Whether we understand it or not, our thoughts significantly impact what we can accomplish. So before you expect someone else to have confidence in your ability, you must have faith in your ability.

Initially, this may not be easy. You may not even be aware of your daily thoughts that could be hindering you from accomplishing your goal. Starting today, begin taking inventory of the things you say to yourself.

Are you being kind? Are you being a cheerleader? Are you judging yourself or talking yourself out of your dreams and goals? Remember that you can't have negative thoughts and get a positive result. You need to affirm to yourself regularly exactly what you want and know it to be true.

From a very young age, I was always made to believe that I could accomplish whatever I set my mind to. I know that this has had a significant effect on my ability to achieve my goals.

When I was a little girl, I was introduced to affirmations, visualization, and vision boards. All of these things significantly shaped who I am as a person and what I've achieved.

When writing my first book, I told my immediate family and friends I would sell lots of books and get media attention. So when I started pitching my book to different media outlets, my faith never wavered.

I knew that it was going to happen. It was only a matter of time. And slowly but surely, my dream began to manifest. Numerous online radio stations, news outlets, and television stations responded to my request to feature me.

Another example is my book signing. I wanted to have a big turnout, but I didn't know a lot of people that I could personally invite. I didn't want to have a typical book signing at a bookstore. I wanted to instead have an after-hours party where people could come and socialize under the backdrop of my book.

So instead of worrying about what would happen, I just set an intention to have a successful book signing party. In the months leading up to my book signing, I had someone reach out to me who'd read *The Buzz*, loved it, and agreed to help me plan my party. Not only did he live in another state, but he'd also never planned a party before because it was a new business venture that he was taking on. So as you can imagine, he was nervous. Funny enough, I had to encourage him to overcome his fear in the days leading up to the event.

Despite never meeting him and the more obvious fact that he'd never planned a party before, I had complete faith that he'd pull it off and told him so every step of the way.

As the weeks grew closer, he began securing sponsors, media, and vendors for the book signing. On the night of the party, we probably had close to a hundred people show up. We had no idea where all those people came from, but the party was a success, and I sold a lot of books!

The point of my sharing these examples is to say have faith in yourself, your projects, your manuscript, and the publishing of your book.

This doesn't mean you won't have bad days. It just means you'll know when to stop sulking, pull yourself up by your bootstraps, and begin working again.

While I consider myself a positive person, I still have days where I'm hard on myself, where I expect more from myself, and where my inner critic creeps in. And on those days, I allow myself to be human. I don't beat myself up and chide myself for having emotions. I allow myself to experience what I need to feel in those moments and then move on.

I look for positive things in my life, things I can be grateful for, and things that are going well. I begin to focus on those things instead of what's not going right.

Having a positive mindset takes practice. Especially if you find yourself surrounded by people who are complainers, negative, don't want more for themselves, and aren't working towards their goals.

Two great ways to become more positive are starting your day with affirmations and ending your day with gratitude. This is something that I could do more regularly, but I have received great benefit on the days I do.

When I wake up, I read my goals, look at my vision board, and read my affirmations. Before I go to sleep, I affirm what I am grateful for. Adding these two practices to your day will significantly change your mindset.

By starting your day focused on your goals, you'll find that you'll be way more intentional throughout the day. It's tough to read your goals and then not do anything throughout the day to achieve them. Ending your day with thoughts about what you're grateful for helps you to experience more positive emotions.

Here are a few recommendations for books that have personally helped me to keep a positive mindset. If you read them, email me at snewell@writeonepublications.com and let me know your thoughts.

Secrets of Success by Sandra Anne Taylor
The Dream Giver by Bruce Wilkinson
E2 by Pam Grout
The Secret by Rhonda Byrne
Think and Grow Rich by Napoleon Hill
Surround Yourself With Doers

Who are the five closest people to you in your life? Are they successful? Are they positive? Have they accomplished the goal you're trying to achieve, or are they supportive of your dream to become a published author?

There was a point when I was younger when I had to assess the people in my immediate circle.

I knew what I wanted for my future, and if that meant cutting out the naysayers, the people who were content where they were, and anyone who didn't want to see me do well, then so be it.

And this doesn't mean you can't be friendly or social. It just means that you are protective of who you spend a great deal of time with, who you share your intimate thoughts and fears with, and who you tell your hopes and dreams to.

Sometimes by default, we carry people from one aspect of our life to another (maybe high school over into adulthood) because we've grown accustomed to them being present, not realizing that growth sometimes alleviates people from our lives. I'm sure you've heard the saying; people come into your life for a reason, season, or a lifetime.

It's up to you to determine in which one of those buckets a person fits. However, I can tell you that having someone in your life that's negative can affect the progress (or lack thereof) that you make in your life.

While in context, I'm speaking about real-life people, you need to be mindful of the virtual people you allow in your life as well. Social media gives us access to old friends, colleagues, extended family members, and strangers. And because sometimes we aren't aware of people's thoughts and opinions, you may inadvertently be accepting someone into your life that's negative, constantly complaining, or posting one negative news story after another.

I can tell you from experience that it can begin to take a toll on you.

I recently had to do a full sweep of my social media because I found that some virtual people I followed were negative and weighing on me emotionally. In turn, it was affecting my creativity, my ability to write, and just affecting my overall mood.

When it comes to family or anyone that you can't necessarily cut out of your life, remember a few things.

Be protective of your dreams and goals. If you know that they aren't going to be supportive, it's okay to keep your goals and plans to yourself.

Deal with people where they are. If someone is negative and you know they aren't going to change, accept them for their good attributes and move on.

Because I work from home and live in a city where I don't know many people, I try to take advantage of networking functions to meet people who are positive and working towards their own goals. Being in the presence of people who are doers keeps me motivated to perform at the level of my peers.

In addition to networking in real life, networking on social media is another great option. You can use social media to put yourself in the company of people who are already successful or in a position you'd like to be in.

For example, on Instagram, I follow pages of people who are entrepreneurs, writers, or just overall positive people. This helps to keep me motivated and focused on my goals when I'm perusing Instagram throughout the day.

Seeing how other people are working toward their goals - the progress they're making, the tools they're using, and the resources they're sharing – is helpful and will subconsciously push you towards your goals.

The basic idea is that no matter where you turn, whether in your real life, online life, the books you read, or the television shows you consume, you want it to benefit your growth. You'll be surprised how small changes affect and motivate you toward your goals.

Who are the five closest people to you?

1. ____

2. ____

3. ____

4. ____

5. ____

Who are five people that you can begin following on social media that will help motivate you?

1. ____

2. ____

3. ____

4. ____

5. ____

Find Someone Who Believes In
You No Matter What

"Writing is a lonely job. Having someone who believes in you makes a lot of difference. They don't have to make speeches. Just believing is usually enough." – Stephen King

Having someone to believe in you is important because there will be days when you are questioning your writing and days when you may even be on the verge of giving up.

You'll need someone in your life, a spouse, a friend, or a family member, to encourage you to keep going. Luckily, I have a few people who believe in me immensely and are all assets to me in different ways. These are people that I can be completely transparent with. I can tell them my fears and concerns, and they listen without judgment.

This will be extremely important for you to have as well. For some of you, someone instantly popped into your head. For others, you may have difficulty pinpointing who can fit into that role. Looking elsewhere is okay if you don't have anyone in your immediate circle who believes in you. Here are some of the attributes you are looking for when looking for a support system:

> ➢ Someone who has accomplished their own goals
> ➢ Someone who already has a successful writing career

> ➢ Someone willing to share their experiences
> ➢ Someone willing to encourage and support you
> ➢ Someone who isn't going to judge you because of where you are currently or because of your mistakes
> ➢ Someone who is positive

As such, here are a few ideas for places you can begin to look for support with your writing:

> ➢ A writing coach
> ➢ Facebook groups for writers
> ➢ Online writing communities
> ➢ In-person writing communities

On the following pages, I will share actionable steps you can begin taking right now to help you specifically with your writing.

Identify Your Goals

Before you begin writing your manuscript, you must identify your goals. This will help keep you motivated to complete your manuscript once you start.

Once you've identified your goals, it's equally important that you read your goals regularly. Otherwise, out of sight, out of mind. Answer the questions below to help you identify your goals:

I want to write a book because…

____

____

____

____

By writing a book, I hope to be able to…

____

____

____

____

I am passionate about this genre because…

____

____

____

____

____

____

____

____

Start Small And Write Often

Perhaps the idea of writing a book is just too much for you to wrap your mind around. Does this sound familiar to you? You sit down at your computer and open a blank page in Microsoft Word, but you have no idea how you will write an entire book, and it becomes overwhelming to you. For those of you who haven't written anything, start small.

> - Write a blog post.
> - Share your thoughts (or micro-blog posts) on social media.
> - Comment on other people's blogs, social media, etc.
> - Write an article on the topic you're passionate about and pitch it to a relevant website.
> - Start a newsletter list where you share your ideas and thoughts with people who subscribe.
> - Write an email and share it with family and friends who will benefit from your knowledge.
> - Write in your journal.
> - If you write fiction, write a short story.

If you already have writing experience and the thought of writing a book still overwhelms you, start small. Try not to think of your project as a book or a specific word count because the idea can be overwhelming. Instead, think of it like this: words turn into paragraphs, paragraphs turn into chapters, and chapters turn into books.

So, write one chapter at a time and only focus on that chapter. Don't begin to think about the road ahead. Instead, just focus on just what's in front of you. It makes the entire process easier.

For example, when I'm writing about writing, I can knock out chapters quickly, and not be overwhelmed because I know the subject inside and out. But when I sat down to tackle the topic of fear, it was a topic that I don't talk about frequently enough that I could crank out numerous chapters.

So initially, I thought, "How many chapters can I write on this subject?"

Once I got over that initial thought, I went right into my process of breaking it down into small steps. I first broke it into ideas I wanted to share, then those turned into paragraphs, which turned into chapters, eventually turning into this book. Make it easy for yourself. Take it one step at a time.

Also, remember that every topic doesn't require an 80,000-word count book. Consider publishing a Kindle or eBook version only. This will take some of the pressure off when sitting down to write your manuscript. The publishing industry has a new saying: "Short is the new long."

eBooks are great for newbie writers because you can break your story into smaller segments, spreading your ideas over a couple of books rather than one large one.

People are busy nowadays and are consuming books in airports, coffee shops, on their phones, and in waiting rooms. Because of this, they don't necessarily have the time to read massive books as they once could. Readers, more than anything, want value and to feel as though they got their money's worth. So if you write a shorter book, ensure that you provide value. And for fiction writers, ensure you have a book that engages your audience.

The other thing you'll need to do is write often. Writing often helps you to:

> Stay in a creative space.
> Get better at writing.
> To get more writing done in each session.
> To complete your book faster.

The more you write, the easier it becomes.

Make Time For Writing

Aspiring writers often wonder how they can make time to write, and rightfully so. With all our adult responsibilities, it seems impossible to make time to write on an already busy day. However, I'm of the mindset that if you want it, you'll make time for it!

Since I've been an adult, I've always had a busy schedule. Like you, I've been busy doing what life demands, like going to school, working, being a parent, and pursuing my dreams.

There were days early in my writing career when I came home from a stressful day at work, cooked dinner, spent time with my son, ran a blog, got ready for work the next day, and then wrote for four hours. On weekends, after tending to my son I'd write in my room because I had ideas for my characters, and I couldn't let the inspiration pass by. There were mornings I went to work on two hours of sleep because the inspiration wouldn't rest. There were days when I was downright tired of my manuscript because I'd read it THAT much. But I still had to make time to write!

Of course, I'm not recommending you go all renegade like I did (unless you want to), but there are easy ways to make time to write throughout your day without compromising any of your responsibilities. These are super simple tips that are going to make you think, "Wait, what? No! No! I need something more scientific."

I'm going to make this easy for you! You can implement these tips as early as today. Now I must warn you that you'll have to make sacrifices if you want to complete a manuscript. And you're going to make a lot of sacrifices if you want your book to be good. I can't promise you that it will be easy, but I can promise you that it's worth it!

Part of the reason we don't make time for writing is that we know that it is a huge undertaking. Writing a manuscript isn't like writing a letter to a friend.

Completing your manuscript will require dedication, research, creativity, and, last but not least, time (and a lot of it). So when time is an issue, how do we conquer it? Break it down into smaller segments of your day!

Use whatever small window of opportunity you can grab until you complete your manuscript. If you have thirty minutes while your baby is down for a nap, take it! An hour while your son is at soccer, take it! A lunch break at work, take it! Take your computer with you and write on the train on your way to work. You'll be surprised at how much you can get accomplished.

Remove the thought from your mind that you need huge blocks of time to write. Think about it like this, even if you write for just thirty minutes, you've advanced your story. Do that enough, and you'll start to see progress! Forget the idea that you don't have the time. Because you do! We all have the same twenty-four hours, and people with lives just as busy as yours have completed a manuscript. And damn it, you can too!

Okay, now that you know how to snatch time from everywhere you can get it, I'll share how to kick it up a notch so you can knock multiple chapters out at a time. This will make the difference in you working on a manuscript for a long time or a reasonable amount of time.

If writing is your passion, consider making sacrifices. I love TV as much as the next person, but I don't watch much of it. I instead use my TV time to advance my manuscript, work on my business, and gain new clients.

Have you ever looked up and realized you spent an hour on social media? Use that time to work on your manuscript instead!

I get it… we all need downtime. But if you're rested, why not use your downtime to advance your manuscript? Make a habit of it, and you'll find that you'll be more creative. You will have more than enough ideas for ways to advance your story.

You will suddenly find the time you never knew you had and have a finished manuscript. Now I've got to warn you, you'll need to isolate yourself during your writing time. Choosing to take time for yourself may make your friends and family uncomfortable. But remember, there's usually discomfort in the things we want for ourselves. In time your friends and family will respect the fact that you need solitude to write.

If you usually sit with your buddies in the cafeteria for lunch, eat at a coffee shop, and spend your lunch hour writing instead. Just think what you could accomplish if you did this five days a week?

Some of you may be considering taking time off from work to write. If you decide to take a sabbatical and write for six months or even a year, use your time wisely. It's incredible how little time you think you have, and then when you get a bunch of it, you flub it all away. You'll need to be disciplined to complete your manuscript because the time will go by quicker than you could ever imagine. But if you have the luxury of taking time away from your full-time job to write, it will greatly benefit you in the long run. Try your best to stick to a schedule and be stingy with your time as if you were working a job. Having periods where you can write will not only help you get more written, but it will also help you become a better writer.

Now there are a few of you that I've still not managed to convince to make time to write. For you, I suggest you take baby steps.

Jot down plot twists, ideas for new characters, and ways to expand the story. When you do have time to write, you'll have an idea of how to get started instead of staring at a blank page. As you see progress, it's easier to make it to the finish line.

I'm speaking from experience. The closer I got to finishing my manuscript, the easier the writing became because I knew I was closer to becoming a published author!

Writing Tips

Now that you have an idea of what you can do to stay focused on your writing goal, I want to share some tips that will make the writing easier.

As a writing coach, I've seen aspiring writers do things that can hinder their process. So in this section, I'm going to share exactly what to do to keep writer's block at bay and keep you from battling the three "p's."

While I've encouraged you repeatedly to start where you are and begin writing, you must have a clear idea of the direction and vision for your book.

Begin researching your book idea to determine whether or not your idea is profitable, what the expectations of the readers of your genre are, and the research that relates to the actual writing of your book. Some of you may be tempted to skip this step, but don't!

What if, from your research, you determine that the topic you want to write about isn't selling on Amazon? Would you still write the book? Would you still spend twelve months of your life writing a book that could only garner a few sales?

It doesn't matter whether your book is fiction or non-fiction, self-help or romance; every book requires research. If research is an area that you're unsure how to start, let me recommend my eBook, *How To Do Research And Write Faster*.

Once you have the research done, begin outlining your book. This will help you identify what should be included in each chapter and will take some of the pressure off when trying to figure out what you will write next.

And lastly, try to stay organized! If you keep all of your ideas on your phone, do that. But if you have notes on your phone, in a journal, and in your email, it makes it difficult to remember these places when it comes time to write.

Another important reason for staying organized and having a clear and concise vision for your book is writer's block. Sometimes writers sit down at their computers, wrongly diagnosing not being able to write as writer's block. When in fact, it's not writer's block at all.

For fiction writers, it's sometimes that they have not identified their plot, sub-plots, or characters. Whereas non-fiction writers may not have adequately identified their book's purpose or what they want to share with their audience.

Writer's block can also be identified as one of the three "p's." This is because it can and will keep you away from your writing for extended periods. So do everything you can to keep writer's block at bay.

Speaking of pitfalls, think about what you're going to do if something happens in your life that requires more of your attention. Are you going to keep writing no matter what? You may need to reduce your writing time, but don't stop writing altogether if you can help it. From my clients' experiences, I can tell you that stepping away from your writing, in most cases, means never finishing your book.

By making a definitive decision now as to what you will do if a pitfall happens, you'll have essentially affirmed that this book is getting written no matter what!

Be okay with making mistakes! This is all new for you. You've never written a book before. You've never published a book. You've never marketed a book. Therefore, you will undergo some things that you just won't have any prior knowledge of. You may make some mistakes. This is fine; it's all a part of the learning process. Don't beat yourself up over it; most of all, don't stop writing!

This may sound cliché but create a sacred writing space. For me, I must be in a clean and well-organized area. I love burning candles or incense; sometimes, I'll even have a cup of green tea. A comfortable space will help you be creative and make you more inclined to sit there and write.

We talked about this earlier, but I want to repeat it, save the editing for the end. When you sit down at your computer, just do a brain dump. Step number one is to get all of your ideas onto your computer. When you get to a place where the ideas aren't coming as fast as they were, it's okay to re-read what you've written. Otherwise, beginning the self-editing process prematurely will only hinder your creativity and possibly send you down the rabbit hole.

Let go of the need for perfection! As I stated earlier, this is something that I struggled with at the beginning of my writing career. Yes, I want you to write well. Yes, I want your book to be amazing! But at some point, you have to write "The End," and take all that you've learned and apply it to your next book. Every book is a new opportunity to write better.

No matter the genre you write, always be authentic. Sharing your thoughts and ideas is scary, and because of this, we may feel the need to write with caution. For instance, if you're a fiction writer and you want to write a sex scene, WRITE IT!

Don't be scared of what people will think of you. Just write the scene authentically.

For non-fiction writers, if you have a viewpoint that goes against everyone else, WRITE IT! That may very well be the thing that catapults you to success. Do you know how boring the world would be if we all thought the same?

Another important thing is to be clear about your target audience. I have talked to countless aspiring writers, and many tell me, "Oh, my book is for everyone!"

Every time I hear this, I want to scream, "NOOOOOO!" and end with a wall slide.

Your book is not for everyone! There's not a book that is written that was written for everyone! Your book is no different.

There is a demographic of people that will benefit the *most* from your book. That group is your target audience. When writing your book, know who your target audience is. Knowing your target audience will help you not only write a book they will enjoy and gain value from, but also allow you to market to them in a way that resonates and makes them want to buy.

And please don't stop learning! Even if you feel like you don't need to read an article because you know the information already, read the article anyway.

I still click on articles about how to write in first person, how to find your target audience, and how to market a book.

Why? Because every writer sharing information on the Internet has a different insight and maybe even a different approach that I may have never thought of.

I will never get to a point where I feel I know everything about a subject. And so it's for that reason that I often click on these articles even though I may already know a great deal about the subject.

Writing requires constant education. That means that you must consistently read your genre, read articles related to writing and publishing, and constantly work toward your goal.

This brings me to my last point - utilize the experts! These are the people that will help you to better your manuscript. These people are beta readers (avid readers of the genre), writing coaches, and editors.

Never feel as though these people don't have value. Each of us, from the beta reader to the writing coach, provides value to the writer differently. While friends and family are great, don't rely on them to give a critique of your manuscript.

Go to the publishing experts. There's always value in speaking to someone who's been there and done that!

These are the people that can tell you whether your book can compete in the retail market, the areas in which you can improve your manuscript, and the areas where you've excelled. As a writing coach, I have so many insights from my experience publishing my books and insights I've gathered from helping countless authors publish theirs.

In conclusion, I hope from reading this book you've addressed your fears and made a decision not to allow fear to stop you from accomplishing your goal.

I genuinely believe that everyone has a story worth sharing. I also think that the people who become published authors are the aspiring writers who've decided to forego their fears and go after their dreams no matter what.

It's obvious that you have a passion for writing or else you wouldn't be so compelled to write. The writing is not going to stop nagging at you; the only thing left to do now is to write. So repeat after me:

I am a writer.
My writing is good enough.
I am creative.
I will finish my manuscript and publish my book.

What you've read in this book has provided you with a head start on your writing career. However, none of what you've learned will work if you don't apply it. So guess what? I'm holding you accountable. Now that you've taken steps to overcome your fear of writing, begin writing.

A Small Favor To Ask…

As you know, reviews play an integral part in our success as writers. Would you be so kind as to leave an honest review of *Write The Damn Book!* on Amazon? As a thank you, please enjoy a sample chapter of my next book, *How To Write Your First Book,* so you can learn the exact formula for writing a successful book.

How To Write
Your First Book

Writing a book can be very intimidating for a first-time author. For that reason, many don't get any further than their idea for fear of the process being too overwhelming. Writing and publishing can be such a steep learning curve that many of the resources available can leave you more confused than when you started. Although well intentioned, a few months of research can leave aspiring writers wondering, how do I get started? How do I choose a topic? How do I outline? How long should my book be? Should I self-publish or traditionally publish?

But what if I could provide you with a blueprint that you could repeatedly use to help you navigate this process quicker and more efficiently? Would that be helpful to you and take you from talking about writing to actually writing? There are many different types of writers, and this book will benefit each of you. Perhaps you are a fiction writer with an idea for a novel or a non-fiction writer who's an expert on a particular subject matter and is looking to take your business to the next level or to extend your brand with a book. What you will read on the forthcoming pages will give you more confidence to begin writing.

This book is a simple and easy-to-use blueprint for the newbie writer who doesn't know how to get started. This book is meant to answer those questions you're too afraid to ask or questions that may seem simplistic but are vital to beginning your writing career.

Because writing and publishing are likely new journeys you're embarking upon, I want you to be armed with as much information as possible without overwhelming you and sending you screaming for the hills. While this book will encourage you to finish your manuscript as quickly as possible, this book isn't about speed. I won't sell you on writing your book in seven days because, let's face it, you're a newbie. Because you are learning, the process may take a bit longer. But what if you could write your first book in twelve months, and it is something you're proud of? Is that something you can aspire to do?

Yes? Then perfect.

To be clear, this book isn't about the writing itself. Many books can provide you with in-depth information on the writing process. Instead, I will share how to go from having a great concept for a book to being published. I want to share this information with you because, at one point, I was you – a newbie writer with no idea how to get started.

Writing has always come naturally to me. However, when I started writing, I had no clue about getting my ideas in a proper format on my computer, how long it should take to write a manuscript, how to get an agent, or even how to market it. I could go on and on, but you get the point. I was clueless about everything.

In *How To Write Your First Book,* I share my challenges and successes in hopes that you will use this blueprint to create, write, and publish your first book. Purchasing this book was your first step toward becoming a published author, so you should be incredibly proud. By reading this book, you'll learn how to:

> ➤ Affirm you are a writer
> ➤ Choose a genre
> ➤ Establish the name you will write under
> ➤ Research your book idea
> ➤ Beat writer's block
> ➤ Make time to write
> ➤ Format your manuscript
> ➤ Determine how long your book should be
> ➤ Cater to your target audience; and
> ➤ Choose between self-publishing and traditional publishing

Making The Decision To Write

A commonality among aspiring writers is their fear of proclaiming themselves as writers or of taking the first step and actually committing to writing. I am going to encourage you to let go of that fear. Fear is paralyzing and will hinder you from making any forward momentum. If I had a dollar for every person who told me they had an idea for a book yet never started a manuscript, I'd be rich!

"What ifs" are a hindrance to creativity and will prevent you from ever becoming a published author. Affirm that you are an author and will complete your book within twelve months and then work toward that goal fervently.

There are many reasons why people don't claim the title of author. Some know that staking a claim to the title requires them to write, which may be a bit intimidating. For others, it may be the stigma that goes along with writing. The image often portrayed in the media is the nerdy reclusive writer who makes very little money.

I often tell the story of the very first book festival I attended. I had so much enthusiasm about my new writing career. Sitting at my table with my books stacked and ready for my first customer, I had nothing but high hopes for my debut release. As I sat waiting, an established author walked up to my table.

"Is this your first book?" she asked.

"Yes, yes, it is," I answered proudly.

I felt she'd been writing for some time, so I asked, "What about you?"

"I've written over 20 books," she said.

Hoping she would provide some guidance and wisdom, I asked her a few more questions, to which she adamantly responded, "If you plan to make money from writing books, then you've chosen the wrong career."

While her comment didn't deter me from pursuing writing, I was disappointed that she wasn't more encouraging.

Obviously, it didn't stop me from pursuing a writing career; however, many aspiring writers are told this and become deterred. It prevents many from seeking to write full-time, or even part-time, for that matter.

If what has deterred you from writing has anything to do with financial compensation, there is some truth to what the author shared. However, as a published author and now a writing coach, there are a few things that I can share with you concerning the monetary aspect of writing that may be helpful. These are things that this veteran author didn't share with me that I wish she had.

Writing is a creative undertaking. It requires a time investment, just like any other career path you embark on. Much like going to school for a trade, you'll need to go to school for writing (so to speak). Whether you participate in writing and publishing courses, read books like this, or use Google as your school of choice, it will require your time. For that reason, you'll have to allow time for your career to blossom.

Being a successful published author is not a goal that will happen overnight. Before deciding to write professionally, I worked for some of the biggest financial companies. Monday through Friday, I would sit at my desk and oversee my client's accounts, and every two weeks, I would get a check that reflected my work. Though challenging in the beginning, after some time, the work became easier. I could oversee the money in my sleep.

Writing is a bit different! Whether you write fiction or non-fiction, it requires you to be creative and present, and in most cases, you write without knowing whether you will be compensated fairly in the end. That's why I encourage writers to ask themselves; is writing my passion? Is this the career I would choose whether I were being compensated or not? If you answer yes to both of those questions, it will be during those days when you're writing your first draft and not being compensated for your time that your passion will propel you forward.

After I embarked upon my writing career, someone I knew shared with me that she'd decided she was quitting her job and going on a sabbatical to write her first book. At this point, I had been away from my corporate job for two years, and I knew what that path consisted of.

My first advice was to ensure she'd acquired a nice savings before she decided to walk away. You'd be surprised how quickly savings dry up when you don't have any income. The second thing I suggested was for her to be stingy with her time. There's something about working from home that makes people assume you're sitting around watching reality shows while eating snacks. Friends and family will begin to ring your phone incessantly. The requests to do them a quick favor will become a part of your everyday routine, and before long, you'll realize that you've wasted your entire day and haven't written a thing.

While I will discuss this more in an upcoming chapter, I wrote my first book while working a full-time job, blogging, freelancing, going to school, and being a mother. If you can maintain your day job, I would encourage you to do so. That way, you won't have the financial pressure you would have if you quit.

That said, here's what I wish the veteran author had told me. Nothing sells your first book like a second book, and nothing sells your third book like your first two books. When I first published my book, I had success. However, even with that success, I still didn't live up to the numbers I thought I would in that first year. Because of that, I became paralyzed and stopped writing, hoping to figure out where I went wrong and to determine why I didn't hit my projected numbers. It took me a minute, but at some point, I realized I'd made a mistake in not continuing to write! I was a new writer with no fan base, and like all the writers that came before me, I needed to establish myself first.

My experience was not unique to me. Countless other writers feel like they didn't make enough money with their first book, and they do just as I did and stop writing. However, if you look at the truly successful writers, they have lots of books on the market. If you seek to write as a career, you'll need to do exactly that – write!

Write enough books so that you can be a success. Writing one book and quitting because you didn't recoup costs or because you didn't make as much as you thought you would, will not put you in a position to be successful.

Lastly, be realistic! This is extremely important. I pursued my passion for writing because I was laid off from my corporate position. If it weren't for that, I don't know that I would have had the courage to step out on faith and pursue this career full-time as I've done. Did it take a level of courage not to go and find another corporate position? Well, yes, on some level, it did. However, I will say that faith has pushed me a good portion of the way.

Also, I'm much happier than I ever was in my corporate position! Writing and helping people is my purpose, and it brings me great joy. You can't put a price tag on that!

So, what allows an author to be comfortable? In addition to receiving an income from writing books, it's essential to supplement your income.

Despite being a great writer, success still takes time. Sure, we've heard of the overnight success stories. These people decided they needed to make ten thousand dollars a month. They then sit down at their computer and crank out a bestseller. But most of us will have to work hard to make that happen. So, consider additional ways to supplement your income while your writing career progresses.

I supplement my income in a few ways. Most of my income comes from my book consulting business, where I coach writers like you to succeed. I also have several smaller streams of income.

First, I started a blog. Initially, I created my blog to build my fan base and promote my book consulting business, but it also helped me gain passive income through advertising. I started a YouTube channel, which again allows me to grow my fan base and promote my business, and I also receive advertising revenue from this medium. I also have a video course that provides an additional income source.

In addition to the books I sell on Amazon, I also have books that are exclusive to my personal websites. Because it's on my own website, I can charge according to the value of my books and not by what everyone else is charging on Amazon.

Think outside of the box! How can you create additional income streams related to your niche or genre? As a non-fiction writer, feel free to use the ideas above as ways you can make extra money. As a fiction writer, you will be able to do a few of these, but it will be vital for you to continue writing.

If you know that writing is your passion and what you seek to do, whether full or part-time, commit to it today. Be realistic in your goals and give yourself ample time to allow them to manifest. Permit yourself to make mistakes, but more importantly, produce quality work. In the next chapter, I will discuss the importance of good quality writing, how it's vital to your success, and how to get your ideas out of your mind and onto your computer.

Did you enjoy this sample chapter? Visit Amazon to purchase a copy of *How To Write Your First Book*.

Need help writing your first book? Schedule a FREE Strategy Session!

CALL NOW!

1-877-859-7483

howtowriteabookthatsells.com

ABOUT THE AUTHOR

Stefanie Newell is the go-to writing coach for first-time writers looking for direction on writing and publishing their first book. Through her writing, publishing, and marketing experience, she helps aspiring writers unleash their authentic voices and share their messages through the pages of their books.

You can find out more about Newell and her company at:

http://howtowriteabookthatsells.com

More Titles From
The Author

How To Write Your First Book

'Need To Know' Writing Terms

Fiction

Fictional literature is made from the imagination. Its purpose is to entertain. With this genre, you read to enjoy. It uses narrative elements such as theme, conflict, characters, setting, and resolution. It gives readers a theme, message, moral, or lesson.

Non-fiction

Non-fiction is literature that is based in fact. Its purpose is to give information. With this genre, you read to learn. It uses text features like the table of contents, glossary, index, labels, charts, photos and graphs. It gives readers information or directions on how to do something.

Self-Publishing

Self-publishing allows a writer to have full control over their book. By handling the publishing of your own book, the author maintains control of all aspects of the decision making process as well as pays all of the costs for publishing the book. The self-published author makes the decisions on the final edits, the title of the book, and the book cover. Self-publishing is for all writers, both fiction and non-fiction, and perfect for every genre.

Traditional Publishing

Traditional publishers are the pioneers of the publishing industry. Once an author is signed, the traditional publisher will front all of the costs for the publishing of your book. In return, they take a percentage of your book sales. Traditional publishing is an excellent route for authors who aren't looking to spend upfront money. Traditional publishers handle the day-to-day business as it relates to your book. Sometimes, the traditional publisher will assist with book signings, radio and television interviews, and any promotional tours supporting your book.

Self-help book

A self-help book is written to instruct its readers on solving personal problems.

Memoir

A memoir covers a specific person, historical event, or thing. The text is about the personal knowledge and/or experiences of the author.

Autobiography

An autobiography covers the author's entire life to the present.

Biography

A biography is someone's life story written by another person.

Antagonist

Antagonists are the bad guys of literature. An antagonist is a person who actively opposes or is hostile to someone or something.

Protagonist

The protagonist is the main character of your book. The protagonist is the one who is living the story you are writing. They are the ones in the middle of whatever conflict you have created. If you are using a first person narrator, it is the protagonist whose point of view your readers are seeing.

POV (Point of View)

The narrator's position in relation to the story told.

First person

A literary style in which the narrative is told from the perspective of a narrator speaking directly about themself.

Third person

Third person limited means that the story is told from an outside narrator who only knows the thoughts of one character in the novel. This third person limited narrator can work exceptionally well because it brings your readers closer to the story's protagonist. Using a third-person limited narrator, you can make your readers feel what your main character feels and question what they question. You can make them feel for your character during the struggles they may face.

Plot

The novel's main events are presented by the writer as an interrelated sequence.

Setting

The place or type of surroundings where something is positioned, or where an event occurs.

Flashback

A scene in a novel set in a time earlier than the main story.

Pacing

Pacing, in fiction and non-fiction, is the speed at which a story is told.

Brainstorming Your Book Idea

Non-fiction writers, begin to put the main ideas of your book into a logical order. What do you want to share with your reader? In what order do they need to know this information?

Fiction writers, begin giving thought to your characters, plot, and subplots. What distinct characteristics do your main characters have? What interrelated events need to happen to accomplish your plot goals?

On the following pages begin writing the first thoughts that come to your mind about your book.

Made in the USA
Columbia, SC
02 November 2024